Rex Weyler

THE VOICE OF THE GALILEAN

The Story of a Life,
a Journey, a Discovery,
a Gift, and a Fate

Manifest is a series of small books that address the important topics and issues of our time, written by activists, philosophers, scholars, and artists. Intended as insight guides for those on journeys of discovery, hope, faith, resilience, and regeneration, they speak truth.

"We plant seeds that will flower as results in our lives, so best to remove the weeds of anger, avarice, envy and doubt, that peace and abundance may manifest for all." - Dorothy Day

[illegible]
THE VOICE OF THE [illegible]
The [illegible] of [illegible]
[illegible]

[illegible] is a series of small books [illegible]
[illegible] topics and issues [illegible]
written [illegible] scholars [illegible]
[illegible]
discovery [illegible] and regeneration [illegible]
[illegible]

"We seek ways [illegible]
[illegible] the words [illegible]
[illegible] peace [illegible]
[illegible] for all." – Dorothy Day

REX WEYLER

THE VOICE OF THE GALILEAN

THE STORY OF A LIFE,
A JOURNEY, A DISCOVERY,
A GIFT, AND A FATE

WOOD LAKE

Editor: Mike Schwartzentruber
Proofreader: Dianne Greenslade
Designer: Robert MacDonald

Cataloguing in Publication data is available from
Library and Archives Canada

ISBN 978-1-77343-155-0

Published by Wood Lake Publishing Inc.
485 Beaver Lake Road, Kelowna, BC, Canada V4V 1S5
www.woodlake.com | 250.766.2778

Wood Lake Publishing acknowledges the financial support of the Government of Canada. Wood Lake also acknowledges the financial support of the Province of British Columbia through the Book Publishing Tax Credit.

Wood Lake Publishing acknowledges that we operate in the unceded territory of the Syilx/Okanagan Peoples, and we work to support reconciliation and challenge the legacies of colonialism. The Syilx/Okanagan territory is a diverse and beautiful landscape of deserts and lakes, alpine forests and endangered grasslands. We honour the ancestral stewardship of the Syilx/Okanagan People.

Printed in Canada.
Printing 10 9 8 7 6 5 4 3 2 1

CONTENTS

What was your word, Jesus?
Love? Forgiveness? Affection?
All your words were one word:
Awaken.

Antonio Machado,
Proverbios Y Cantares, 1912

PART 1

IN SEARCH OF A HISTORICAL JESUS

> We can, at the present day, scarcely imagine the long agony in which the historical view of the life of Jesus came to birth.
> – Albert Schweitzer, *The Quest of the Historical Jesus*, 1909

This short book seeks the most likely authentic teachings of a genuine, historical Jesus, Yeshua ha Nazorean, a Jewish peasant, who became a renowned teacher and healer in first-century Palestine.

We know from our 20th-century perspective that Jesus became the central figure in what is now a global religion with over a billion adherents.

I grew up in a secular home with a Catholic mother and Protestant father, attended grade school with Jewish friends, and attended university where I met Hindu, Buddhist, and Muslim adherents, agnostics, and atheists. I learned to respect people's beliefs and traditions. I also learned to be rigorous about understanding history.

Our precious world has witnessed enough sectarian and religious violence to compel us to ask whether religion actually inspires moral behaviour. Common citizens everywhere, even without religion, know how to treat people with respect, while on the other hand, religious doctrine is relentlessly employed to justify violence.

Religious tolerance remains a hallmark of civilized society, but pandering to religious hypocrisy does not. The Western world needs the authentic voice of Jesus, as much now as it did in the first century. We need to overcome the gap between the original teachings of Jesus – seeking one's inner light and showing compassion for others – and the long history of violence and abuse in some Christian traditions: for example, the horrifying Inquistion, wars between Catholic and Protestant sects, and the shameful abuse of children in Christian residential schools.

The time has long since arrived for modern society to reckon with the misuse of religion. In the West, perhaps it is time to rediscover what Jesus, a poor Jewish peasant from Galilee, actually said.

HOW DO WE KNOW?

As we examine the historical record to find an authentic Jesus message, we will pose the historian's questions: Who says? Who corroborates the story? What credentials does the witness possess?

The historical name of Jesus, for example – Yeshua ha Nazorean – provides a useful place to start. The Hebrew and Aramaic languages do not contain the "J" letter or sound. Yeshu and Yeshua were comon names that make reference to the Hebrew god. In Greek, Yeshua became Iêsous, translated to Latin as Iesus. The "J" was added by English translators in the 16th century. The term Nazoreans does not likely refer to a town of Nazareth. There exists no historical evidence for a town of Nazareth in the first century. Nazareth is not mentioned in the Old Testament, Paul's letters, the Talmud, or by ancient historians before Constantine's church historian Eusebius in the fourth century. The linguistic evidence in the gospels suggests the title "Yeshua *the* Nazorean," not "Yeshua *from* Nazareth." The Hebrew root *Nazar* means to abstain, set apart, or consecrate. The Nazoreans were an ascetic sect who practiced pure living, "set apart" in their religious purity.

"Some of the words attributed to Jesus were not actually spoken by him," writes Robert J. Miller, editor of *The Complete Gospels*. "While this is not news to scholars, it is news to the...public." During the last century, historians and text scholars have developed advanced methods of analyzing language to reveal layers of borrowing and revision in ancient manuscripts. The Matthew and Luke gospels, for example, appear to copy Mark and a mysterious early collection of sayings.

Over 200 verses common to Luke and Matthew are not copied from Mark but are so nearly verbatim that they cannot be explained by coincidence. Scholars believe the Luke and Matthew authors lifted these passages from a common source. German scholar Johannes Weiss labelled this lost collection "Q" signifying the German "quelle," meaning "source." The Q sayings likely appeared by 50 CE in Galilee.

Startling new texts – the gospels of Mary,

Thomas, Philip, and others – have risen from their desert graves to provide fresh sources of Jesus sayings. Some 200 significant historical accounts contribute to the search for the sayings and deeds of Jesus, taking us far beyond the boundaries of the New Testament gospels.

Jesus wrote nothing, spoke in Aramaic, and his voice survived decades of oral transmission before written records appeared. The earliest surviving complete manuscripts of popular gospels appear three centuries after Jesus' death, in Greek.

TO WITNESS THE TRUTH

Only about 30 papyrus manuscripts and fragments prior to the fourth century attest to the words and deeds of Jesus. Today, paleographers generally believe the oldest manuscript evidence of a New Testament story is a famous little scrap of papyrus, about the size of a cash register receipt, called "P52," held by the Rylands Library in Manchester, England. Handwriting analysis links the scribe to the era of emperor Hadrian, 117 to 138 CE. The fragment contains 110 legible Greek letters forming 12 complete words and 20 partial words.

As we look back into history for the earliest

indication of Bible stories in the first three centuries after the life of Jesus, the evidence breaks up like so many islands disappearing into the mist. The Rylands papyrus P52 represents the last pebble in the surf on the last islet. The front side of P52 reveals the following, roughly, rendered in English:

us Jew
no one that the w
id signify
die ent
rium P
and say
ew

Scholars have filled in the presumed missing letters and words to parallel a passage that appears in the Gospel of John, 18:31, in which Jesus stands before Pilate:

> Pilate said to them, "Take him yourselves and judge him according to your law." The Judeans replied, "We are not permitted to put anyone to death." This was to fulfill what Jesus had said when he indicated the kind of death he was to die. Then Pilate entered the headquarters again, summoned Jesus, and asked him, "Are you the King of the Jews (Judeans)?"

There appears a significant leap from fragment to gospel, but the available words and letters fit well enough with later Greek manuscripts that most scholars feel confident P52 parallels the passage in John. Actual gospels, based on early stories and sayings collections arrived much later.

In 1840, at the University of Leipzig, 25-year-old Bible scholar Constantin von Tischendorf grew frustrated in his attempts to translate the Greek New Testament. No two Greek New Testament sources agreed, and von Tischendorf recognized "many errors" in manuscripts. He suspected some editors "did not shrink from cutting out a passage or inserting one." In April 1844, von Tischendorf embarked for Egypt, "to discover some precious remains of any manuscripts ... which would carry us back to the early times of Christianity."

At the foot of Mount Sinai, at the Monastery of St. Catherine, he found a basket filled with old parchments, goatskins inscribed in uncial Greek, all capitals, without word breaks or punctuation. Tischendorf dated the documents between the fourth and eighth centuries. Among the parchments, Tischendorf discovered an Old Testament, described in his memoirs as "one of the most ancient that I had ever seen." In 1859, he returned and discovered a complete Greek manuscript of the New Testament and most of the Old Testament. These manuscripts became known as Codex Sinaiticus, the oldest known complete copy of the Bible, dating from about 350 CE.

We recognize a significant leap across three centuries from the execution of Jesus in about 30 CE, to the tiny P52 remnant composed around 125 CE, and finally to the earliest complete Bible manuscripts from 350 CE. We may well wonder, then, how accurately the stories were preserved.

As we follow the trail of stories from the voice of a living Jesus, across three centuries to the appearance of gospel manuscripts, we encounter missing pages, edited passages, conflicting accounts, and faulty translations.

The tiny P52 fragment reveals the challenge scholars face when interpreting incomplete evidence. This fragile scrap of history depicts a simple Galilean peasant hauled before the most powerful politician in Judea. On the reverse side of the fragment, scholars discovered the earliest known physical evidence of a quote attributed to Jesus. Here are the surviving words and letters in English:

this been born

rld that I bear
s the true
says to him
and this
to Y
any

The "Y" suggests Yeshua, or Jesus. Scholars extrapolate these clues to parallel John 18:37–38. "So you are a king?" said Pilate. This appears as a trap, but here Jesus exhibits an earthshaking power of character: "You're the one who says I am a King," responded Jesus. "This is why I was born and this is why I came into the world: to bear witness to the truth."

When confronted with life or death at the hands of a tyrant and a mob, this vulnerable, human Jesus coolly deflects adulation, and offers up modest dignity in its place. By simply bearing witness to the truth, Jesus – whether historically or mythically – exposes for history the cowardliness and duplicity of his tormentors. The statement, allegedly from Jesus, suggests a leader who stood up to power and possessed a sublime wit. This response also suggests the ideal attitude – "witness the truth" – with which to launch an investigation into his authentic teachings.

EXCAVATING JESUS

We have seen that history's earliest manuscript fragments depicting Jesus appear a century after his death. Historians believe certain documents appeared earlier than the physical evidence, based on language style and other clues. Scholars work with two dates for each scrap of evidence; the date of the manuscript itself, and the presumed date of an original, based on language clues.

Between 90 and 120 CE, historians place the Gospel of John and the Gospel of Mary; the Apocalypse of James; an epistle attributed to Barnabas; letters by the first Christian patriarchs; and writings from rival Yeshua movements led by Valentinus in North Africa, Marcion on the Black Sea, and the Ebionites east of the Jordan River.

As we push back in time to the previous decades 80–100 CE, the gospels of Matthew and Luke appeared, along with the Dialogue of the Saviour; the Gospel of Peter; the Egerton Gospel, an independent narrative of Jesus; and a New Testament letter attributed to Jesus' brother James, defending the poor against statements by Paul that favoured the upper classes.

Still earlier, from 60–80 CE, historians place

the Gospel of the Egyptians, a dialogue based on the Thomas sayings; the original Gospel of Mark, ending with Mary Magdalene fleeing the tomb of Jesus; and an Egyptian fragment, Oxyrhynchus 840, in which Jesus debates Pharisees about washing "the outer layer of skin" while ignoring inner righteousness. At this time, a Christian acolyte wrote the Letter to the Colossians, later attributed to Paul, preaching faith in the messiah and denouncing Jewish traditions. Thus, we see that even within 30 years after the death of Jesus, congregations of followers clashed over his legacy.

Finally, if we claw back through the record to the very earliest dates for which paleographers estimate the existence of documented Jesus sayings, we find precious few accounts from the first three decades after his life, from 30–60 CE. The authentic letters by Paul likely appeared around 50 CE or shortly thereafter, and announce Jesus as the messiah. The Gospel of the Hebrews, likely composed in Egypt between 50–60 CE, depicts the divine preexistence of Jesus, his life, and his post-death appearance as the incarnation of divine Wisdom, the goddess "Sophia." Three short fragments known as Papyrus Egerton appeared in Syria in the mid-first-century, and depict Jesus scolding hypocrites, who, "honour me with their lips, but their hearts are far distant."

These lines, taken almost verbatim from the Book of Isaiah, are later repeated in the Matthew gospel. Here we reach as close as the evidence takes us to the survivors of the Jesus movement, and already we hear of hypocrisy and conflict.

Scholars believe the earliest "first layer" of Thomas and the Q axioms appeared by 50 CE around the Jordan River, in Galilee. The parallel sayings in the relatively early gospels – Thomas, Mark, Luke, and Matthew – suggest a core Jesus message that we might summarize as,"Find your inner light, share it with the world, give to others, eschew wealth, shun violence, avoid rules, and heal the sick."

AN ELUSIVE JESUS

Searching outside Christian texts for early – pre-fourth-century – evidence of Jesus provides precious few accounts. Among first- and second-century historians, who do not mention Jesus at all, we may count Plutarch, Livy, Seneca, Philo, Judaeus, Dio Chrystosthom, and dozens of others. None of the 870 Dead Sea Scrolls, composed during the two centuries before, during, and after the life of Jesus, contain a single reference to Yeshua, a Galilean teacher.

However, in the year 112 CE, Pliny the Younger, the Italian governor of Bithynia on the Black Sea, writing to Roman emperor Trajan, mentioned "Christians" and reported their custom of sharing a common meal and promising to commit "no theft, or pilfering, or adultery." Pliny does not mention Jesus – the Latin *Iesus* – but only "Christus," an anointed one. Eighty years after the death of Jesus, Pliny does not mention him by name and appears to know nothing about him.

The Jewish Talmud of that era offers nothing about Jesus, but the Babylonian version of the Talmud mentions one "Yeshu" in a passage about proper procedures for a stoning.

> On the eve of the Passover Yeshu was hanged ... a herald went forth and cried, "He is going forth to be stoned because he has practiced sorcery and enticed Israel to apostasy."

The full passage suggests this Yeshu held some political connection with authorities and had five disciples, Matthai, Nakai, Nezer, Buni, and Todah – details that don't precisely match the

Christian version of Jesus, although some scholars believe this might refer to Yeshua ha Nazorean.

Roman historian Tacitus, in his *Annals* of 115 CE, provides the earliest unambiguous secular reference to Christus as a historical person in Judea. Writing about Nero in 64 CE, Tacitus says the following:

> [H]e falsely charged with guilt, and punished Christians, who were hated for their enormities. Christus, the founder of the name, was put to death by Pontius Pilate, procurator of Judea in the reign of Tiberius.

Jewish historian Flavius Josephus wrote *The Jewish Antiquities* in about 90 CE. In the only extant copies from much later, two short passages in Books 18 and 20 mention "Iêsous." However, most scholars consider these to be later additions placed into Josephus' history by Roman church historian Eusebius.

Scholars have no copy of the Josephus manuscript before the Middle Ages, by which time Christian editing of historical documents was common. Some scholars believe the language in these passages appears inconsistent with the aristocratic Josephus, and more like the voice of a later Christian theologian.

Church historian Eusebius quotes variations of these alleged Josephus references to Jesus, suggesting that several versions existed. Scholars, therefore, widely suspect Eusebius inserted these passages into Josephus' manuscript. In the 17th century, the Bishop of Norwich, Richard Montague, acknowledged that the Josephus passage was probably a later Christian addition.

After reviewing the secular references to Jesus in the first three centuries following his death, we are left with Pliny's account of Christus, and Tacitus, who links Christus to an execution under Pilate in Judea, consistent with the papyrus fragment P52.

We may feel shocked that we possess so little from early secular historians about Jesus, and that we learn absolutely nothing from these scant references about his actual teachings. We might presume that his words and deeds inspired the common meal and ethical lifestyle observed by Pliny, but we do not gain from the early historians a single quote to aid in our quest for the authentic teachings of Jesus.

A HISTORIC JESUS

In the 18th century, German philosopher Hermann Samuel Reimarus launched the "quest for the historical Jesus," asking what teachings from the surviving record can be traced to the historic Jesus. Eighty years later, David Friedrich Strauss published *The Life of Jesus Critically Examined*, attempting to distinguish legend from history. Strauss pointed out that the mythologizing of heroes does not imply that the hero never existed. On the contrary, Strauss believed the scattered praise for Jesus in different contexts suggests that he did exist.

Meanwhile, in America, Thomas Jefferson, a devout Christian, took his scissors to the Bible to extract "the gold from the dross," as he wrote to first U.S. Surgeon General, Dr. Benjamin Rush:

> [F]ragments only...come to us mutilated, misstated, and often unintelligible...disfigured by the corruptions of schismatizing followers ... perverting the simple doctrines he taught, by engrafting on them the mysticisms of a Grecian sophist, frittering them into subtleties, and obscuring them with jargon.

To lawyer and diplomat William Short, Jefferson wrote the following:

> I find many passages of fine imagination, correct morality, and of the most lovely benevolence; and others, again, of so much ignorance, so much absurdity, so much untruth, charlatanism and imposture, as to pronounce it impossible that such contradictions should have proceeded from the same Being.

In 1906, German Calvinist minister Albert Schweitzer published *The Quest of the Historical Jesus* as an effort to extract the ethics of Jesus from later doctrine. Schweitzer concluded that the gospels embellished the original message with the religious ideas of a later age. Schweitzer felt that church leaders were not prepared to accept the upheaval that would follow from making a distinction between a historic Jesus and the messiah of Christian faith. Unwilling to confront the church, he let the historic question rest, took up medicine, and spent the remainder of his life living the teachings, as he understood them, by healing impoverished African villagers at his hospital in Lambaréné, Gabon.

Since the work of Schweitzer, hundreds of

scholars have taken up the search for historic evidence regarding Jesus. Modern research by these historical, archeological, and text scholars reveals that careful textual analysis can identify the most likely core teachings of a historical Jesus. (See appendices for the list of those I referenced.)

THE ESSENCE

This search for an authentic Jesus message has followed rules of evidence used by historians. We scrutinize the records for corroboration by the earliest independent sources. We consider general historic convergence, for example, which sayings reflect social conditions of first century Galilee and Judea. We identify passages borrowed from ancient lore and those reflecting later language and doctrines.

The earliest known sayings collection, the Greek Logia Iêsous, includes six sayings from Thomas that match the Q verses from Matthew and Luke:

> Seek and you will find.
> Seek the light within you.
> Share your light with the world.
> Before you judge others, notice the impediment in your own eye.

Don't worry about your clothes and comforts.
Beware religious authorities, who take the keys to knowledge but don't enter and don't let you enter. Be sly as a snake, gentle as a dove.

We can start here to define a core message. When we look at the confluence of the Q verses with both the Thomas and Mark gospels, we find nine shared sayings and three additional shared themes, in different versions, paraphrased here.

The kingdom is like a mustard seed, small, but it grows naturally into something useful.
The kingdom is not in the sky, but here and now, found in self-knowledge.
What is hidden, will be revealed.
Place your light on a lamppost; don't keep it hidden. Speak out. Help others.
What you put into your mouth does not defile or purify you, but what comes out does. Bring forth good fruits.
Make the two into one and move mountains.
The first will be last.
Those who have will get more. Those with nothing are deprived.
To enter a strong man's house, you must bind him first, and then enter.

Here are the three common Thomas-Q-Mark themes:

> Ask and you will receive; seek and you will find.
> Your sins are forgiven, as you forgive others.
> A disciple's mission: remain simple and humble, go to towns, share food, heal, give what you have, and tell people, "This is the kingdom."

We have seen that Jesus also repeated common wisdom sayings:

> The Golden Rule: Treat others as you wish to be treated.
> Love your enemies.
> It is the sick who need a doctor, not the healthy.

Jesus did and said much more, but these ideas form the core of his teachings. John Dominic Crossan developed a method of cataloguing Jesus themes or "complexes," not necessarily verbatim language, from multiple texts. Crossan identified subjects such as "The Mustard Seed," "Kingdom and Children," "Mission and Message," and so forth, ranked them based on chronology and sources, and published his results in his 1991 book *The Historical Jesus.* Most of these themes, aphorisms, and parables likely appeared within the first 30 years after the execution of Jesus, with three or more independent sources:

The Kingdom is like leaven in bread.
Blessed are the poor, the sad, the persecuted.
Split wood, lift a stone, and I am there.

Let the dead bury the dead: commit now.
The first shall be last.
If slapped on the cheek, offer the other cheek.

The Sower: Seeds cast onto good and bad soil.
The Good Samaritan: Compassion makes one a neighbour, not authority or religion.
The Coin: Give the emperor what belongs to the emperor; give to God what belongs to God.

In 1985, Robert Funk convened 30 scholars at the Pacific School of Religion in Berkeley, California, to address the question of authentic Jesus sayings. Funk's "Westar Institute" continues to meet twice a year as the "Jesus Seminar," made up of over 200 international scholars. They have published results of their work in hundreds of academic papers and popular books including *The Five Gospels* and *The Complete Gospels*.

These scholars do not presume to be infallible, but provide rigorously informed opinions based on strict, published rules of evidence. Among the highest ranked items on the lists compiled by Westar's Jesus Seminar, we find the familiar sayings and themes outlined above. Matthew and Luke both place several of these sayings in the Sermon on the Mount and the Sermon on the Plain, respectively. Scholars place the essence of these sermons at the heart of Jesus' teachings. Among the top ten items on the Jesus Seminar rank of likely Jesus sayings, seven are found in the Sermon on the Plain:

Blessed are the poor.
Blessed are the hungry.
Give to anyone who asks.
If someone asks for your coat, give your shirt also.
If someone asks you to walk a mile, walk the second mile also.
If slapped on the cheek, offer the other cheek.
Love your enemies.

These seven lines alone make up a radical social agenda. We've heard them so often we may take them for granted, but imagine living by these precepts. For Jesus, righteousness and sin are the fruits of personal action, not the result of ritual or convention. Self-reflection and humility form the core of Jesus' personal advice, while non-aggression and generosity form the core of his social platform.

The Q sayings include this unequivocal duty: "Give to everyone who begs from you." Similar lessons in generosity appear in the legends of Socrates, Buddha, and Lao Tzu, but Jesus introduces this unrestricted munificence to the Jewish tradition. The Greek Cynic philosphers relinquished possessions and mocked the pretensions of the wealthy, but they did not incite active social reform. Jesus did. Jesus turned spiritual philosophy into social action.

In the famous story of the Good Samaritan, a lawyer asks Jesus, "So, who is my neighbour?" at which point Jesus tells the story of a travelling Judean, robbed, beaten, and left for dead beside the road. A Jewish priest and a Levite pass by but ignore the victim. A Samaritan, typically considered a foreign enemy of Judeans, takes pity, cleans the man's wounds, and puts him up at an inn. Who is a neighbour? The neighbour is not necessarily someone of the same culture or religion – and not someone with spiritual pretensions – but rather the person who demonstrates compassion with action. This answer would have sounded radical in first century Judea and remains a lesson the world still appears to need 2000 years later.

The Apocryphon of James, or "secret writing of James," attributed to Jesus' brother, was likely composed in the early second century. Like the Ebionites, the author rejects Roman Christian authority and denies that Jesus' death represents atonement for sins. Rather, this author believes that the "kingdom of heaven" exists within. Jesus is quoted, speaking to James and the disciples.

> No one will ever enter the kingdom of heaven at my bidding, but only because you yourselves are full ... Unless you receive this through knowledge, you will not be able to find it ... know yourselves. For the kingdom of heaven is like an ear of grain after it had sprouted in a field. And when it had ripened, it scattered its fruit and again filled the field with ears of another year.

A letter attributed to James also appears in the New Testament, defending a life of good work against the Paulist doctrine of faith.

The religion that is pure and undefiled before God, the Father, is this: to care for orphans and widows in their distress, and to keep oneself unstained by the world ... Can faith save you? ... faith by itself, if it has no works, is dead ... I by my works will show you my faith.

PART 2

A Voice in Galilee

> In his ethical code there is a sublimity, distinctiveness and originality ... If ever the day should come and this ethical code be stripped of its wrappings of miracles and mysticism, the Book of the Ethics of Jesus will be one of the choicest treasures of the literature of Israel for all time.
>
> – Joseph Klausner, *Jesus of Nazareth*, 1922

Wisdom is the currency of peasants as well as scholars, perhaps more so. Jesus, poor and disenfranchised, absorbed the culture around him, distilled it, and revitalized it. He probably heard wandering mystics and sages from as far away as Asia.

As a Jewish peasant boy in Galilee, young Yeshua almost certainly heard about Hillel or perhaps studied with him directly. The fact that he put a twist on Hillel's version of the Golden Rule distinguishes Jesus. The way he applied Cynic shrewdness or Asian philosophy to life under Roman and Judean authorities suggests a virtuosity of language and social instinct.

In the authentic historical record of Jesus, the Aramaic Yeshua, we sense a discrete personality radiating an exceptionally luminous humility and intelligence. After his encounter with John the Baptist, Jesus reframed his mentor's idea of a righteous kingdom: We create a divine kingdom here and now by finding our own inner light, by speaking out, and by helping others.

Jesus mediated the kingdom of God through action. Rather than wait for justice to come from God, he attended to the dispossessed peasants in the real world. Historical evidence shows that Roman authorities, temple priests, and Herodian overlords, interpreted his actions as threatening. He knew the fate of John and offered hope to the poor, knowing full well that the rulers in Jerusalem would resist him violently.

Like great visionaries before him and since, Jesus awakened from the cultural trance of his age and from the conventions of society. We can be fairly certain that he experienced a spiritual epiphany, which provided him with the motivation for his life's work. Thereafter, he saw before him suffering humanity, envisioned a better world, and set out to manifest that vision. The authentic Jesus, or Yeshua the Nazorean, brought heaven to earth in the here and now.

Although his message rings clear, authentic words from the lips of Jesus remain elusive. One must be prepared to dig, compare texts, verify witnesses, and to discriminate honest accounting from innocent mistakes, predisposed mythmaking, and prejudicial manipulation. We also must remain cautious regarding the tendency to reshape historic heroes to serve our own ideas. We must, in simple terms, witness the truth.

After his life, a new, Romanized status quo absorbed and revised his legacy. Claims of authority, promises of salvation, and threats of damnation dominated later accounts and did not require the historical Jesus. Conversely, understanding his acts of compassion and singular wisdom *does* require an appreciation of this authentic person.

The Jesus who actually walked the earth – the Galilean peasant, healer, sage, rebel, and teacher – gave himself to the world. His teachings belong to humankind, as do the teachings of Lao Tzu, Vandana Shiva, or Martin Luther King. No one owns these teachings or possesses any particular authority to interpret his message. The sayings, parables, and lessons of this Jewish mystic enrich world heritage, and any scholar or curious reader may enjoy access to the insights, warnings, and pleadings of this brilliant and compassionate observer of humanity, who lived 2,000 years ago.

Serious scholars understand that Jesus wrote nothing, his ideas circulated by word of mouth, and the absolute details of his history have been obscured by later accounts. Nevertheless, historians reconstruct a reasonable sequence of events by comparing Jesus stories to each other and to the public record of the age. The following description summarizes what historians believe are the most likely events in the historic life of the Jewish peasant, Yeshua ha Nazorean.

THE ACTS OF YESHUA

In about 4 BCE, before the death of Herod the Great, Yeshua, "God's promise," first opened his eyes on Galilee, born to a mother Miriam, whom we know by the modern, European

"Mary," by a father Yosef, or perhaps by an unknown father. Jesus had four brothers – Yacov (James), Yoses, Yudas, and Simon – and at least two sisters (possibly Miriam and Salome). His childhood remains obscure. Birth and infancy accounts appear late in the record, contradict each other, clash with known history, and reflect popular motifs about divine births. Jesus, almost certainly, was not born in Bethlehem or anywhere in Judea. His later sayings reflect a Galilean cultural heritage.

He grew up in a northern Israeli cultural tradition, although his heritage may have been mixed, and his influences appear diverse. In thinking of Jesus as a "Jew," we must differentiate between Galilean peasants and Judean urbanites and notice that he consistently rejects Jewish social convention. He lived and taught near trade routes between the Mediterranean and the East, and his teachings reflect the worldly ideas of his era.

Jesus first appears in history as a disciple of John the Baptist, a renegade prophet with a following in the wilderness east of the Jordan River. The relative assurance of this derives from later attempts to recast Jesus' relationship with the famous and much-loved John, who forgave sins for free in defiance of the Jerusalem priests' monopoly, drew crowds, and paid with his life on the orders of Herod Antipas. After John's execution, some of his disciples became followers of Jesus, who attracted other devotees, both men and women.

Jesus' transformative epiphany appears to have stimulated profound insight, and thereafter Jesus radiated extraordinary charisma. He adopted Capernaum as a second home, but remained an itinerant teacher. He travelled the regions around the Sea of Chinnereth (Sea of Galilee), possibly reaching Sidon on the northwest Phoenician coast, Caesarea Philippi in the northern hills, and Gadara across the Jordan River to the southeast. He may have travelled east across Persia.

Jesus spoke in private homes, public squares, and in the countryside. He primarily addressed a Jewish peasant audience, but he accepted all races and persuasions of followers. He consorted with social outcasts, the poor, the sick, and even the despised tax collectors. He directed his audience to enter the kingdom through self-awareness and righteous action. He held communal meals as part of a central ritual. People believed in his healing powers, which likely contributed to his success. He cured a lame man in Capernaum, where scholars accused him of wielding the power of demons.

High-ranking Pharisees were not common in Galilee. Nevertheless, Jesus probably did confront religious authorities serving the Jerusalem temple hierarchy. He openly confronted those who presumed to speak on behalf of God and chastised them for hypocrisy and failure to help the people. Such authorities would have expected miraculous signs from any real prophet, which Jesus refused to display on demand. On the other hand, the crowds who flocked to him expected healings and the benefits of communal sharing, which they received. His fame spread throughout the region.

Sometime during the reign of Roman emperor Tiberius, around the year 30 CE, and during the spring festivals, Jesus entered Jerusalem, perhaps on a donkey, symbolizing Jewish peasant rebellion against foreign oppression. In Jerusalem, he attracted crowds of devoted followers and his popularity embarrassed the temple elite. He likely shared a final communal meal with his closest followers. The evidence suggests that someone close to the movement betrayed him, although the name "Judas" may be a fiction used to blame Jews. Irritated authorities arrested him and executed him. The details of his trials and execution remain obscure.

Only the Roman prefect, Pontius Pilate, possessed the authority to order his death. Pilate, a notorious thug, not the ambivalent moralist later portrayed for a Roman audience, would have executed Jesus without so much as a shrug, as he did with other rebel leaders. An order from Pilate to neutralize troublemakers in Jerusalem during Passover would have been carried out with ruthless precision. Roman soldiers tormented Jesus, marched him to "Golgotha," or "Skull place," outside Jerusalem, and executed him. Being efficient, the Romans almost certainly executed others with him. Meanwhile, his male supporters avoided attention, while his mother Mary, Mary Magdalene, Salome, and other women witnessed his suffering and attended to the body.

Some of these details may not have happened as they appear, and other recorded details may bear some historical truth, but this account outlines what we can reasonably say – based on the earliest, corroborated records – about an authentic Yeshua of history. All the rest remains highly speculative or transparently invented. Some stories about Jesus are borrowed from other sources: divine birth, blood atonement, conversations with demons, and the spring sacrifice and rebirth of "the righteous one."

After Jesus' death, his brother James, Mary Magdalene, and fisherman Simon Peter emerged as leaders among his disciples. James held an important position in Jerusalem and possibly among the Ebionites. The Gospel of the Hebrews depicts James as a leader, and the Thomas gospel has Jesus naming him as his successor. James was executed in 62 CE by high priest Ananus, an event recorded by Jewish historian Josephus.

Considerable evidence suggests that Mary Magdalene enjoyed some special relationship with Jesus, that she deeply understood the teachings and adopted them in practice. No evidence confirms a marriage, although accounts, such as the Gospel of Philip, have Jesus kissing the Magdalene. Mary likely anointed Jesus in a ceremony of peasant kingship, became an accomplished disciple, and sustained the teachings after his death. She likely resurfaced in Egypt, and based on later legends, possibly reached Ethiopia and southern France.

Later accounts portray Jesus variously as a rebel, a prophet, a Greek-style hero, a wise sage, a Cynic philosopher, a healer, an anointed king, and a saviour. He appears more modest in his own descriptions of himself as a "Son of Adam," a human. Among his poor neighbours, he made the promised kingdom accessible. His work would have demanded unworldly courage in the face of imperial oppression. Local Roman collaborators and Herodian sycophants did not want their privileged lives spoiled by a zealous preacher from Galilee exposing hypocrisy and stirring up revolution.

MULTITUDES

All histories are reconstructions. Every piece of surviving evidence about Jesus reflects a later individual or group *impression* of what he said and did. We possess not a single first-person claim by an eyewitness to the life of Jesus. The Gospel of Thomas comes close by claiming, "These are the secret sayings that the living Jesus spoke and Didymos Judas Thomas recorded," but even so, some Thomas passages are second-hand, some echo common lore, and others appear as later additions.

Crossan, one of the most highly respected scholars of Jesus history, points out that our search is encumbered by three "giant filters," since ancient history was recorded by 1) the elite, 2) the literate, and 3) by males. We mitigate these biases by understanding oral peasant culture and women's voices.

Finally, we must overcome our own biases and hopes that history conforms with our private viewpoint. Jesus Seminar scholars warn, "Beware of an idea of Jesus that is too congenial to you." Jesus disturbed the status quo of his time, so we should not be surprised that he occasionally disturbs us. We may find ourselves simply mystified: How is the divine kingdom like a cracked jar?

Our historical mission, to the extent possible, is to arrive inside history, to witness events from the era's own perspective, and to understand Jesus and his followers not from the 21st century – or from the fourth or 15th centuries – but from the first century, through the dust of ancient streets and through the eyes of peasants yearning for a better world. The characters we wish to know – Jesus, Mary Magdalene, and the others – were humans, struggling with very real needs, fears, and hopes. To know them, we must look behind the metaphors and mythologies to discover the authentic human experience.

Around the Mediterranean, during the four centuries after Jesus, the Roman hierarchy burned libraries and outlawed certain beliefs in an effort to control the human story, culminating in Emperor Constantine's state religion. The heirs of the Roman Empire have attempted to manage knowledge and religion ever since, advancing the notion that there exists only one, orthodox way to experience or articulate spirituality.

Much of what became Roman Christianity, and later Protestant Christianity, can be traced to pagan, Egyptian, and Persian sources adopted by Paul, Justin Martyr, Constantine, Eusebius, and Augustine, not by Jesus. Paul, who had persecuted Jesus followers, introduced the messiah tradition into the written record. The historical Jesus virtually disappeared from second- and third-century "Christianity." Furthermore, many modern Christian rituals, such as Easter, reflect medieval rituals borrowed from ancient pagans, recalling Ishtar, Asherah, and spring planting rites.

There exists no evidence that Jesus ever claimed to be a diety or implied, "believe in me and you'll go to heaven." He never claimed that his mother was a virgin. He never instructed disciples to create an institution and hierarchy of priests, to accumulate wealth, or curry power. He did not advance the Augustinian idea that his followers should go to war on behalf of God. In fact he counselled the exact opposite: nonviolence, simplicity, modesty, and direct generosity.

We have seen that Jesus' aphorisms and parables circulated orally among independent congregations – Ebionites, Egyptians, a "Q" community, Mark and Matthew communities – and that some congregations compiled anthologies of sayings and stories embellished with folklore and legend. These gospels endured three centuries of editing until some were rejected and others assembled as a canon in the fourth century. Scholars identify traces of an authentic Jesus in dozens of other documents, including Dialogue of a Saviour, the gospels of Philip and Peter, the Egerton and Egyptian gospels, and in the mystic poem "The Thunder: Perfect Mind."

The Mary gospel – which appeared in Greek by the early second century – serves this discussion because it represents the earliest known account of Jesus from a woman's point of view, otherwise purged from the historical record. From Mary we hear familiar Jesus ideas in a unique voice: "The seed of true humanity exists within you. Follow it!" The "mind is the treasure" that "sees the vision." We hear that all forms in nature co-exist with one another and that the mature soul is one that has "slain" the desire and ignorance that binds it to despair. These passages may reflect worldly ideas of the era, but they also record an authentic feminine perspective of Jesus' teachings.

We find the most genuine core of Jesus' message in the earliest editions of three collections, namely Thomas, Mark, and the Q (Quelle, or "source") sayings. We have seen that a fair summation of this core message survives in the famous Sermon on the Mount and Sermon on the Plain in Matthew and Luke, respectively, drawn from the earliest Q layers. Although scholars do not agree on every line, the most likely authentic sayings emerged from textual analysis during the last two centuries. Although Jesus' message has been redacted and obscured, any curious and rigorous seeker may discover the key threads that make his teachings unique and relevant.

By comparing and contrasting these sources and weighing chronology, corroboration, and historical convergence, we can identify the essence of what a radical, Aramaic-speaking, Jewish Jesus, Yeshua, might have said to an assembled crowd in Galilee. Imagine the multitudes gathering on a mount or on a plain, by the seaside, in a village square, or crammed around the courtyard of a private home. Mary, Thomas, Peter, and other close disciples would sit nearby. Infirmed peasants would press around him. Jesus would be tired, dusty, and wearing a ragged tunic, yet his eyes would shine with uncommon brilliance and his voice would reverberate with earthshaking courage and charisma. He possessed no script but would react to the events around him.

In such a setting, the historical Yeshua might say something like this:

A VOICE IN GALILEE

You wish to be healed and forgiven for your sins, and so it shall be, but my dear friends, you don't know how lucky you are. You are fortunate to be poor and hungry. Your suffering brings you closer to the true kingdom of God. The rich are distracted by pleasures and power. Look, they stand away at a distance. They will gather up more riches and you will be deprived, but you are the lucky ones.

The kingdom cannot be bought. Nor is it something grand that will come tomorrow and be handed to you. Here, this is the kingdom. These children. Be like these innocents. See? Their kindness is natural. The kingdom is for ones such as these. It is like a tiny mustard seed, almost invisible, but look how it grows wild in the fields and provides a home for the birds and little animals.

Seek this kingdom in yourself. Look within. There is a light inside, and if you look, you will find it. Everything hidden will be revealed to those who seek. When you find this light, don't keep it to yourself. Who would light a lamp and then put it under a basket? Shine your light from the hilltops. Speak out. Tell others. Do as we do.

Look. We have nothing. No staff, no food, no extra clothes. Don't worry about what you will eat or wear. Look at the birds. See these lilies. They don't slave away or worry, yet they are fed and adorned more gloriously than the kings. Your father in heaven loves you as much as those birds and flowers. Accept what is given to you from this bounty and take care of others. That is the divine kingdom on earth.

The lawmakers say we have sinned because we healed our neighbours on the holy day. We have no day of rest. Even the birds have nests and the foxes have their holes. Yet a human has nowhere to lay one's head. The holy day was made for us; we weren't made to serve the holy day.

Those of you with two good ears had better listen.

Do you want to live in this kingdom? Then don't call me master, but act on what I am telling you. Don't just hear these words but do as we do. Go among your neighbours, share whatever you have, give to anyone who asks. You can heal the sick yourselves. Tell them the kingdom is here.

But don't act like those who pretend to speak for God, who parade around in fine robes, and demand the best seats in the synagogue. These priests take the keys to the kingdom but they won't enter and they won't let you enter. Don't be fooled. Be sly as a snake but gentle as a dove.

I swear to you, I ask no one for authority. I speak from what I know myself. Love your enemies. Pray for them. Share even with those who rebuke you. If someone strikes you on the cheek, offer them the other. If someone wants your coat, give your shirt also. If you are ordered to walk a mile, go another mile also. What do you care? You have nothing. What can they take from you?

Have you not heard: Treat others as you wish to be treated? Be merciful and forgive others, just as you wish to be forgiven. Don't take your neighbour to the court of law. Settle your disputes among yourselves. You know in your heart what is right and wrong.

And don't judge your neighbours. Before you point out the splinter in your friend's eye, maybe you should think about the timber in your own eye. Do you see? Can the blind lead the blind?

Wake up. Look around you. The kingdom is here, spread out over the whole world and some people still don't see it. Imagine a merchant who gets a huge shipment of goods, but inside he finds a perfect tiny pearl. Wouldn't he want to keep the pearl for himself and sell everything else? The kingdom is like that. It is like a treasure buried in a field. The landlord has no idea, but you can have that treasure.

Be generous, not just to your family and neighbours, but to anyone in need. A man was robbed and beaten on the road and left in the ditch. A priest and a Pharisee just walked by and ignored him. But a Samaritan passed by, cleaned his wounds and put him up in an inn. So who is your true neighbour?

Look. You know who is righteous. What someone puts into their mouth doesn't defile or purify them. What comes out of one's mouth defiles or purifies. Don't just wash the outer layer like the priests and forget the inside. Make the inside like the outside. This is the kingdom. You create good and evil by what you do. Goodness comes from the good that a person builds up in the heart from living a life of common decency. Evil comes from evil work stored up in the heart. Those who try to save their life will lose it. Don't gather treasures that will only be lost. Store up treasures that remain.

Don't worry about sins. Even the lawyers can't tell you what sin is. Sin comes when you act contrary to your nature. But when you know yourself, when you follow your nature, that is righteousness. Male or female are one. In the kingdom there is no male or female.

Start now. Do you think you cannot take up a holy life until you have raised your children or buried your parents? Don't wait. Let the dead bury the dead. Commit now. A slave can't serve two masters.

Beware. Your own family may cast you out, but look at us. We have each other; this is our family.

In the kingdom, the first is last, the last is first. This little child, pure in spirit, is greater than the prophets. Who has something to eat? Bring it out. Share it with your neighbour. The kingdom is here.

SIN AND PURITY

Nothing in this message requires a miracle or supernatural belief. Jesus never defines "God" for his audience, other than referring to "Abba," a "father" in heaven, who will provide sustenance. The only term he uses for "God" in the Sermon on the Mount is "the highest." Listeners in the crowd may have harboured various ideas about deities, but still could have understood and adopted his message to love their enemies and give to anyone who asks.

Recall that both John the Baptist and Jesus addressed four concerns important to first-century peasants: purity, atonement, authority, and acts of righteousness.

Jesus consorted with outcasts, not only the poor, but with tax collectors and sinners. One common, first-century tradition equated sin with the body, sex, and specifically with women. Jesus rejected this and accepted women among his disciples, a policy every bit as radical in his culture as healing on the Sabbath. In the Gospel of Thomas, he equates sin to hypocrisy when he says that if you simply perform rituals, without good deeds, "you bring sin upon yourself."

The Mary gospel provides an invaluable balance against the overwhelming elite, male voices that drafted the orthodox canon, and especially the malicious, patriarchal voices that later excluded and demonized women. The earliest record, the Gospel of Thomas, names only Thomas, Peter, Matthew, James (Jesus' brother), and two women: Salome and Mary. The Sophia of Jesus Christ counts seven women and 12 men among the disciples. The second-century Apocalypse of James reports "seven women" and adds that Mary possessed advanced understanding of the teachings. On the other hand, the canon gospels introduce the tradition of exclusively male disciples.

The evidence of Pliny in the second century records women as "deaconesses" among Christian groups. Second-century Christian leaders Marcion and Valentinus honoured Mary and Salome as disciples, and appointed women priests. These practices so thoroughly clashed with both Jewish and Roman social convention that they suggest a special origin, going back to Jesus, who treated women as equals.

According to the gospel record, a woman, likely Mary Magdalene, anointed Jesus with oil from an alabaster jar, earning praise from the teacher. Peasant followers would have naturally associated her with "the people's queen," the daughter of Asherah, the Queen of Heaven. In the Gospel of Thomas, Jesus answers a disciple about entering the Kingdom: "When you make the two into one...the inner like the outer...male and female into a single one...then you will enter [the kingdom]."

Jesus interpreted purity as a consequence of self-knowledge and public action, not observance of religious ritual. His spiritual epiphany appears to have revealed to him a sacred state of being, whereby both men and women move beyond the precincts of gender.

ATONEMENT

For Jesus, if sin does not follow from breaking religious laws, then those laws do not confer atonement, or forgiveness. Jesus made forgiveness immediate and unconditional. Without relying on religious status, Jesus would say, "Your sins are forgiven." His simple prayer to "Abba" in heaven asks only that one be forgiven "as we forgive others."

In modern Pennsylvania, on October 2, 2006, a disturbed young man, Charles Roberts, entered a schoolhouse in Nickel Mines and shot 11 Amish school girls, four of whom died. The horrified community met on the evening of the shooting with mental health counsellors to process their grief and support their traumatized children. Then, without hesitation, they organized a horse-and-buggy caravan to visit the Roberts family, the parents of the shooter, with food and condolences. The Amish may appear strange to some people, since they reject technology and live simply, but in doing so, they preserve the lifestyle instructions of Jesus. Likewise, they preserve his fundamental message: love your neighbour, even your enemy. Like Jesus, the Amish in Pennsylvania broke the cycle of revenge with forgiveness.

Jesus taught that unadorned, unconditional compassion is the kingdom made manifest. By forgiving, one is forgiven. We have seen that the two most common images Jesus used to describe the kingdom are the tiny mustard seed and the leaven in bread. The kingdom is something small and natural that grows to produce profound effects. Politically, first-century listeners might have interpreted such images as religious rebellion. Ethically, the images might suggest humility and perseverance. Both leaven in bread and the tiny mustard seed represent something small, almost invisible, that grows into something substantial. The wild mustard growing in a landlord's neatly sown field also reflects resistance to oppression.

In the Jewish scriptures, leaven is only mentioned in its absence, as a sacrifice to mark Nissan, the spring equinox, when the Passover lamb is eaten with bitter herbs and unleavened bread. So this image from Jesus would sound radical to devout Jews. The mustard seed would sound radical, in contrast to the Jewish image of the giant cedar with massive roots and expansive canopy. Jesus urges his listeners to safeguard that infinitesimal kernel of understanding until it grows naturally into something that will have impact in the world.

Matthew and Luke gospels record Jesus saying, "the kingdom has come" and "the kingdom is among you." From the Thomas gospel we hear that god's kingdom is both "within you," and "spread out on earth." The hidden will be revealed when we know what is in front of our face. A common first-century view espoused by John the Baptist and later by Christian writers held that God's own divine action would, some day, bring about the kingdom. Statements by Jesus, therefore, that the kingdom is available here and now sound original to him. Whatever Jesus believed regarding El, Yahweh, or Abba, he rejected waiting around for deities to do the work.

It will not come by watching for it. It will not be said, "Look, here!" or "Look, there!" Rather the kingdom is spread out upon the earth and yet people don't see it.

Jesus asks those who will listen to help transform the world now, by helping the disadvantaged. Those who equate spirituality with transcending the physical world in space or time miss this important lesson. Authentic spirituality appears everywhere in nature – "turn over a stone; I am there" – and in the quality of attention that each individual applies in the most mundane of acts. This message remains relevant today.

Those of us who can afford the time to write or read books are the lucky ones. Two-thirds of humanity lives in poverty and nearly a billion destitute people barely cling to survival. Nine million starve to death every year, 25,000 per day, most of them children. Meanwhile, two percent of humanity owns half the household wealth. Indeed, as Jesus foretold, the rich got richer, and the poor continued to suffer. In this regard, we might view 2,000 years of social progress as rather undistinguished. The modern skid-row corner mission offering a soup kitchen, free clinic, and encouragement to the homeless might be the most Jesus-like Christian institution to survive two millennia of cultural evolution.

Giving hope to the disenfranchised remains as politically unpopular today as it was in the first or 12th centuries. We still hear the comfortable and powerful dismiss advocates for the poor as "bleeding hearts," or worse, implying something sinister or criminal in compassion. We have made human greed our economic doctrine.

In the first Jesus healing story in Mark, set in Capernaum on the Sea of Galilee, Jesus tells the paralytic "your sins are forgiven," just like that, without ritual or pretense. This bold assertion of forgiveness removed the power of atonement and healing from the priests and handed it to the poor themselves. Jesus confronted the system of privilege and patronage, inciting the prying scholars at the scene to wonder who gave Jesus the right to forgive sins.

PERSONAL POWER

Jesus, like John the Baptist, healed on his own word, based on his own knowledge. He did not hold a licence from the temple priests or claim to speak for God. Jesus broke the priests' monopoly by healing on his own personal conviction. He instructed disciples to move among the villages as he did, helping those in need. These emissaries had glimpsed the light inside and offered it to others without reservation.

Jesus put his own stamp on healing in three important ways. First, he gave it away without obligation, without asking his beneficiaries to honour him as their patron. "Don't call me master, do as I do." Second, he encouraged disciples to heal others, creating a network of healed healers. Rather than claim special powers, he handed his gift to others, sharing the power before it corrupted his purpose. Finally, he healed on his own authority, without appealing to religious convention or divine sanction. Jesus offered free, universal, unbrokered compassion.

Had Jesus remained in one place, say Capernaum, and established a school as did teachers Hillel or Honi, his enterprise might have brought beneficial economic spinoff to the community. He would have become a patron for his disciples, who would, in turn, have become patrons for others. However, Jesus rejected the entire web of imperial patronage and the commercialization of peasant life in Galilee. He didn't apply for a foundation grant, design a logo, and register his method as a trademark. He gave his kingdom away to all.

His itinerancy was neither forced nor idle, but rather a central living example to follow. The disciples were not wandering around scamming free meals. Jesus taught them to decline all trappings of privilege: family, social, or imperial. Jesus spoke of family conflict as well as social conflict for the seeker of righeousness. Jesus appears to have rejected family hierarchy and privilege that helped promulgate injustice. He rejected family and social practices, for example, that conferred on a father the right to sell his daughters into slavery or to murder his children for believing in a foreign deity.

Jesus' itinerancy reflected an absolute refusal to allow his message to become a public franchise or an economic hedge fund for his friends. Instructions to his most ardent followers remain clear: No money, no extra possessions, no staff or sceptre. Give it up. Heal each other. Share your food. Share whatever you have. Inspire others to do the same. Then, move on and provide healing and sustenance to the next person that needs help. This mission implied a radical response to oppression, violence, and social privilege, and it remains a radical response today. His unique and inspired courage provides one of those signatures that bears witness to a living, walking Jesus. This is not typical, mythological courage. What we witness in Jesus is living, breathing courage.

Rare is the person who achieves fame and does not attempt to leverage the power into some other personal benefit. Jesus was such a person, exhibiting egoless power. He did not exalt himself or send his audience to holy scripture for insight; he sent them back to their own experiences, thoughts, and desires. The authority that Jesus assumed derived from personal knowledge, and he directed his listeners to seek their own personal knowledge.

Self-reflection appears as a motif of the Jesus message in Mark, Thomas, the Q sayings, the Gospel of Mary, Dialogue of the Saviour, and other accounts. See the timber in your own eye. Look within. In Mark, Jesus explains his parable about seeds that fall on poor or fertile ground: "The final group ... are the ones who listen to the message and take it in and produce fruit." The Mary gospel says, "The seed of true humanity exists within you." In Thomas, Jesus says, "When you know yourselves, then you will be known, and you will understand that you are children of the living Father. But if you do not know yourselves, then you live in poverty."

Still today, one might observe real human tragedies driven by the insatiable ego, old habits, resentments, and vengeance. Self-awareness provides the remedy to these obstacles of the ego and represents timeless wisdom. Jesus talks about seeing the reflection of one's self that existed "before you were born," a common image in Vedic and Buddhist traditions. Jesus may have heard about self-knowledge associated with Socrates or Gautama Buddha, but typically he put his own spin on it. Jesus told disciples that when they look inside, they will find a "light," and he encouraged them to impart this light to one's neighbours.

Finding this light is not an intellectual process, but rather intuitive; it is a quality of attention, not a doctrine to be memorized. For Jesus, self-knowledge is not a private concern, but the beginning of a public concern. Self-awareness is the first step in being an effective agent of social justice in the world. With this, we reach the heart of the matter. For Jesus, authentic spiritual insight appears in the quality of one's action in the world. Spirituality is measured by the consequence it produces in the living world.

ACTION HERE AND NOW

The itinerate, modest, culture-crashing style of Jesus emulated the Cynic sages, but Jesus and his disciples were not out to simply mock wealthy hypocrites or score philosophical points. The Jesus mission intended to actually make life better for others by healing them and teaching them to share whatever they had.

The instruction to give freely is particularly interesting since Jesus spoke primarily to the poor. He encouraged them not to dwell on their own poverty and troubles, but rather to give to others. Giving to others appears in Jewish scriptures – Ezekiel, Deuteronomy, and Job – but again, Jesus adds his own emphasis. He provides the example of the Good Samaritan, giving unconditionally. Even sinners love their families and friends, he says; that's nothing special. Be better than that. Love foreigners, those with other beliefs, even those who rebuke and attack you.

When Jesus speaks of love, the Greek manuscripts predominantly use the word *agape*, from the root *agan* meaning "much," signifying abundance and sharing, quite distinct from *eros*, "romantic love"; *phileos*, "friendship"; or *storge*, instinctual "family love." Jesus spoke Aramaic, so we may not know his precise term, but Greek translators used *agape*, love expressed as sharing. Some English translations render this as "love," but we should note that it means "to share." For Jesus' first-century audience, his instruction would imply sharing God's natural gifts, the abundance of the world, distributed equitably to all.

Landless peasants in Galilee had been dispossessed from this gift and they lacked basic food for survival. Jesus showed people that giving rather than hording provided enough for everyone. In large crowds, he instructed his disciples to share whatever food they had, and indeed, no one went hungry. Later writers recorded these events as miracles, and perhaps in some sense they were. Even today, it might appear miraculous if people in a large modern city broke out in generosity, feeding the hungry on a daily basis.

Although Jesus experienced a spiritual awakening, he remained a man of earthly purpose. As much as he borrowed from philosophers and ethical teachers, he was not satisfied with philosophy or ritual. His central point remains unambiguous; spiritual insight is revealed by deeds. Talk is cheap. Action counts. In Matthew we hear, "Wisdom is vindicated by her deeds," echoing a common axiom that Jesus could have heard from an uncle or a wandering sage. Nevertheless, he made the principle his own by becoming a living example.

The so-called Golden Rule – treat others as you wish to be treated – may represent the most common piece of ancient wisdom in the world, and Jesus likely heard it since childhood in the Hillel version – "What is hateful to you, do not to your neighbour" – which Hillel called "the entire Torah." Recall that Jesus flips this around, making it positive and active: "Whatsoever you wish others should do to you, do so to them." Consistently, Jesus asks for action, for physical evidence of understanding. The Buddhists refer to such enlightened action as "achieving the meaning."

Of course, this is no small task. Love those who rebuke us? Who among us can face insult or physical abuse without dreams of revenge? How often have organized Christian churches failed this simple mandate? Witness the Inquisition, witch burnings, the violence of modern empires, or the cycle of revenge in the Middle East. Jesus taught action, but not violence. "Turn the other cheek," he insisted. No violence or warfare anywhere, anytime, honours the authentic Jesus. The papal armies of Innocent III and the U.S. "Corpus Christi" nuclear submarine represent insults to his memory. Unconditional generosity is the challenge Jesus set before the world. Jesus did not have to invent this idea, since it appears as common wisdom, but actually living it became his great gift to the future of humanity. A simple act of unconditional kindness is the tabernacle of Jesus' message.

WITNESS YOURSELF

On the morning of December 21 – the first day of Hanukkah, eve of the solstice, and five days before Christmas in 2003 – I muted the television news commentary and watched the blinking images of cluster bomb victims in the al-Dora neighbourhood of Baghdad. The street scene reminded me of my only visit to Baghdad many years earlier: the yellow-grey stone; homes with dirt floors; and dusty, timeless, sandalled citizens at the mercy of history by the Rivers of Babylon, the great city of Hammurabi and Nebuchadnezzar, the plunder and playground of Cyrus and Alexander. Now, as then, generals whispered secrets of state inside the gates, which retainers would deny in public. I watched the modern empire stagger after desert riches and global supremacy and I imagined all the armies that had forded the Euphrates River searching for power. I remembered standing before the massive stone tomb of King Cyrus, 600 kilometers to the east in Persia, bearing witness to the cold fate of colonial pride. Empires fade, great kings turn to dust, but the human story and struggle for survival endures.

History matters because it tells us how we arrived in our present circumstances and how we might respond. History is the evidence that verifies or refutes social philosophy. Doctrines come and go, harboured by the status quo, drafted to protect power, and parroted to justify self-interest. Truth remains elusive, as any serious student of history knows. Certainty remains the realm of ideologues. "The whole problem with the world," wrote Bertrand Russell, "is that fools and fanatics are always so certain of themselves, and wiser people so full of doubts." The lessons of history cannot be found in lists of rules but might be glimpsed as a distant ship passing in a fog.

Official history gets dressed up to serve the culture that writes it. The counter-history of every age springs from those who are not intimidated by the consequences of acting on their conscience: Jesus, Gandhi, Rosa Parks. Like other innovators, Jesus cracked open the cultural inertia of his age with pure authenticity and unadorned compassion for humanity. Rare is the spiritual experience that cuts through social convention to reveal raw, unprogrammed awakening. Jesus the Galilean, Yeshua ha Nazorean, appears to have experienced just such an epiphany. He found his neighbours drunk on illusion, but few thirsty for knowledge. He exposed the hypocrisy of privilege and offered hope to those left out, the dispossessed, the "losers."

To understand our past, we cannot set the historical issues aside and simply cling to mythologies of former ages. Nor can we set aside the mythologies to understand the historical facts. Truth emerges from both stories and factual evidence. We don't do Jesus or ourselves any service by accepting shoddy fourth-century scholarship, translation mistakes, or politically biased rewrites as the real message of Jesus. Ideas have their time in history, and the time has certainly arrived in the 21st century to honour Jesus as any other historical figure. Regardless of what I or you or anyone believes about Jesus or Mary Magdalene, they deserve honest inquiry. We don't dishonour Jesus by asking hard questions. Did he really exist? What did he actually say and do? What did he believe or intend? On the contrary, such questions are precisely what Jesus would expect. Like the victim of a dysfunctional family, society has failed to know its own history, unable to escape the double bind of the lie itself and the taboo against talking about it.

I recently attended a literary conference in Victoria, British Columbia, and delivered a seminar on "writing history." After the seminar, in the hallway, an attendee asked if I would talk to her about the history of Jesus, and we went to a coffee shop. She appeared curious, but cautious and even distressed. We talked for about an hour and I gave her a list of authors and books to read – Crossan, Karen King, Rosemary Ruether, the Nag Hammadi Library – and some websites to visit. Finally she gazed at me with a look of panic and asked, "If I read these will I lose my faith?" I did not know what her faith was, so I could not answer her question. I felt helpless. If I could see her now, I would like to say, "If you believe that your God created you, including your intelligence, then why would you ever fear using that intelligence to learn about the world or about someone else's religious ideas? What is there to fear in knowledge?"

Spiritual insight may be a private affair, but we all share the same pool of spiritual wisdom recorded throughout history. We have nothing to fear from knowing about Rama, Gaia, Jupiter, Jesus, or Mohammed riding Buraq the white horse into heaven. Even if we learn that certain legends are mythology, not history, we will find that they still reveal secrets about human experience and emotion. The stories *mean* things, important things about how people cope with one another and with the world. We do not have to confuse myth with history to absorb its treasures. We are not stuck in an intellectual limbo, where we "can't prove or disprove" alleged miraculous events that appear in cultural myth. We make such judgments every day to distinguish fact from fiction and genuine insight from delusional madness or manipulative despotism.

Furthermore, we do not serve the memory of Jesus by denying the dark side of religion, the horror of children abused in religious institutions, the victims of the Inquisition, or the casualties of sectarian violence in Belfast or Jerusalem. We often don't talk about religion's shadow because we do not want to offend, but our silence buys suffering. Perhaps if we achieved a better relationship with our own religious traditions, we would find the insight and courage to make peace with other traditions. Ethics are not about beliefs, but rather about the actual experiences of joy or anguish. Our actions, not our doctrines, count in the world.

History is not on autopilot but emerges as the summation of choices and actions performed by the living. "What will be, will be," is a proverb for laziness. "What will be" is the result of the choices we make and actions we take. Jesus lived and taught this lesson. How we act to our neighbour, our enemy, to the unfortunate, to the earth itself, measures our humanity. Jesus encouraged his audience to awaken. Witness yourself. Witness what is before your eyes. Be as a child, alive with wonder and natural generosity. We honour Jesus when we distinguish his teachings from the proclamations of Paul, the machinations of Constantine, or the historical revisions of Eusebius. We cannot have it both ways. There is no historical or cultural value in pretending that the mythic constructions of Roman sycophants or the clever rationalizations of Augustine are a substitute for Jesus.

The historical problem with the later 16th-century Reformation is that it did not reform any of these previous errors or the brutality and pretense of the Romanized revision of Jesus, but only divided the power structure and carried on with atrocities and counterfeit doctrines. The time has come for a *real* Reformation, a simple return to the authentic message of Jesus. Dominican scholar Matthew Fox has written that a "New Reformation will be Interfaith ... female with male ... It will worship a God that loves creation." A real Reformation would worship creation itself. We will learn that spirit and matter are not at war with each other as Plato and the Gnostics surmised and as patriarchal rulers proclaimed. That spirit comes from matter – that is the wonder of wonders!

We live inside the miracle every day, but we miss it with preoccupations to control nature for our advantage. Jesus warned that those who seek to save their lives will lose life. Our modern ecological crisis is a crisis of spirit. Humanity sought salvation in all the wrong places and forgot to worship the one great gift set out before us, the abundance of the natural world. While we cobbled together promises of paradise, we bought and sold the earth's bounty. We have decimated half the the forests that once existed, burned the petroleum, depleted the fish, scattered our toxins, turned farmland into desert, and now we melt the icecaps, dragnet the ocean bottom, and wage war to squeeze the last drop of oil from stone. We appear as little more than the great Babylonian or Roman empires, with fancier technology and a longer reach.

Jesus had faith in humanity, and this knowledge bolsters my faith in humanity. It may take a miracle, or a complete disaster, but perhaps humankind can rediscover simple living, common decency, everyday compassion, and reverence for the earth. We do not need mythic superheroes; we need ordinary heroes who will witness the truth and speak up for those deprived of a voice. Perhaps the living presence of Jesus – the peaceful dream of the Ebionites, Cathars, and Quakers – will endure. Perhaps this presence appears in the actions of Iqbal Masih, the 12-year-old, murdered for opposing child slavery in Pakistan; or in Mairead Corrigan, who marched for peace in Ireland; or in the courage of Gandhi or Rosa Parks.

PART 3

APPENDICES

1. The core Jesus sayings
2. Misconceptions: Sayings and ideas that Jesus did not originate or say
3. Sources

1.
THE CORE JESUS SAYINGS

In what follows, you may notice the similarity between
1. the Thomas, Mark, and Q sayings from the earliest record,
2. the Crossan list, and
3. the Jesus Seminar list.
These three different methods of arriving at authentic Jesus sayings arrive at roughly the same conclusion, and help us identify the most likely core, original sayings.

THOMAS, MARK, AND Q

1. The kingdom is like a mustard seed
Thomas 20; Mark 4:30–32; Q (Matthew 13:31–32; Luke 13:18–19)
"The kingdom...is like a mustard seed. It is the smallest of all seeds, but when it falls on prepared soil, it produces a large plant and shelter for birds of the sky." (Thomas)

2. Don't hide your light
Thomas 33; Mark 4:21; Q (Luke 8:16, 11:33; Matthew 5:15)
"No one lights a lamp and puts it under a basket or in a hidden place. Rather, one puts it on a lampstand so that all who pass will see its light." (Thomas)

3. The hidden will be revealed
Mark 4:22; Thomas 5–6; Q (Luke 12:2, Matthew 10:26)
"There is nothing hidden that will not be revealed." (Thomas)

4. The rich get richer:

Who has receives, who has nothing is deprived This is probably a common maxim used by Jesus.

Thomas 41; Mark 4:25; Q (Luke 19:26; Matthew 25:29)

"To those who have, more will be given, and from those who don't have, even what they do have will be taken away." (Mark)

5. Action, not ritual

Thomas 14; Mark 7:15; Q (Matthew 15:11)

"What goes into your mouth will not defile you; rather what comes out of your mouth will defile you." (Thomas 14)

Good Fruits Thomas 45; Q (Matthew 7:16, 12:33; Luke 6:44)

"You'll know who they are by what they produce." (Matthew 7:16)

6. Unity from duality, two into one, move mountains

This widely attested maxim was likely common lore. The "Faith moves mountains" version is a Paul adaption (1 Corinthians 13:2), not Jesus language.

Thomas 48, 106; Mark 11:22–23; Q (similar idea in Luke 17:6)

"When you make the two into one, you will become children of Adam (human), and when you say, 'Mountain, move,' it will move." (Thomas 106)

7. Entering a strong man's house

Thomas 35; Mark 3:27; (Luke 11:21; Mathew 12:29) Matthew and Luke may have copied Mark, thus only two sources.)

"One can't enter a strong person's house and take it by force without tying his hands." (Thomas)

8. First and last

Thomas 4; Mark 10:31; Q (Matthew 20:16; Luke 13:30)

"The last will be first and the first last." (Matthew)

9. Kingdom is not in the sky, but is here before you
Thomas 3, 51, and 113; Mark 13:21; Q (Luke 10:16); and Mary 4:3–4
"The kingdom...will not come by watching for it. It will not be said, 'Look, here!' or 'Look, there!' Rather the Father's kingdom is spread out upon the earth, and people don't see it." (Thomas 113)

10. Ask, seek, and knock, and you will find
Thomas 2, 92, 94; Mark 11:24; Q (Luke 11:9–10); Mary 4:7; P. Oxyrhynchus 654:2; Gospel of the Hebrews 4; Dialogue of the Saviour.
"Seek and you will find." (Thomas 92)

11. Mission: travel to towns, without money, and heal
Precise instructions vary but Mark, Luke, and Matthew agree: Go among the towns without a bag, money, or second tunic; stay with whoever takes you in, and heal the sick.
Thomas 14; Mark 6:7–13; Q (Luke 10:4–11; Matthew 10:5–15)

12. Blaspheming the Holy Spirit won't be forgiven
Thomas 44; Mark 3:28–30; Q (Luke 12:10; Matthew 12:31–32); Didache 11:7
"Whoever utters a word against the son of Adam (humanity) will be forgiven, but whoever blasphemes against the holy spirit won't be forgiven." (Luke)

EARLIEST, WIDELY ATTESTED SAYINGS FROM THE J. D. CROSSAN INVENTORY

(21 ideas from Jesus recorded before 60 CE with three or more independent sources)

Dominic Crossan examines "complexes" – shared ideas, not direct quotes – based on early evidence and the number of sources. He includes events, although this list includes only original Jesus sayings. Notice the overlap with the Thomas and Q sources. For the full Crossan list, see Crossan's *The Historical Jesus* (HarperCollins, 1992). These are the ideas, according to Crossan, most likely spoken by Jesus.

1. Mission and message
(no money, go to towns, heal the sick)
Thomas 14; Mark 6; Q (Luke 9:1, 10:4; Matthew 10:7–14); 1 Corinthians, Dialogue of the Saviour

2. Ask seek knock
(and you will receive)
Thomas 2, 92, 94; Mark 11:24; Q (Luke 11:9; Matthew 7:7–8); Gospel of the Hebrews; John 14–16

3. Kingdom when and where
(not in the sky, but here)
Thomas 3, 51, 113; Q (Luke 17:23; Matthew 24:26)

4. Who has ears should listen
(likely a common expression)
Frequent in Thomas, Mark, Matthew, Luke, and Mary

5. Receiving (rejecting) the "One who sent me"
Mark 9:36; Q (Luke 10:16; Matthew 10:40); Didache; John 5, 12, and 13

6. Against divorce

Some scholars believe this is later Christian, not from Jesus.

Mark 10:10–12; Q (Luke 16:18; Matthew 5:31–32); 1 Corinthians (Paul); Shepherd of Hermas

7. Defilement

(not what goes into the mouth, but what comes out)

Thomas 14; Mark 7:14–15; Q (Matthew 15:10–11; Acts 10:14, 11:8b)

8. Kingdom and children

Thomas 22; Mark 10:13–16; Matthew 18, 19; Luke 18:15–17; John 3–5

9. The world's light (a light within)

Thomas 24; P. Oxyrhynchus 655; Matthew 5:14; Dialogue of the Saviour 14, 34; John 8, 11, 12

10. Prophet's own country (get no respect)

Thomas 31; Mark 6:1–6; Matthew 13:53–58; Luke 4:16–24; John 4:44

11. All sins forgiven

(blaspheme and atonement) Some scholars believe this is later Christian, not from Jesus.

Thomas 44; Mark 3:28–30; Q (Luke12:10; Matthew 12:31–32); Didache 11:7

12. Blessed the womb (that has not conceived)

Thomas 79; Q (Luke 11:27–28); John 13:17; James 1:25

13. Forgive us as we forgive others (prayer)

Mark 11:25; Q (Luke 11:4; Matthew 6:12–15); plus Clement and Polycarp letters

14. First and last

Thomas 4; P. Oxyrhynchus 654; Q (Luke 13:30; Matthew 19, 20; Mark 10:31)

15. Hidden made manifest

Thomas 5, 6; P. Oxyrhynchus 654; Mark 4:22; Q (Luke 12:2; Matthew 10:26)

16. The sower

(seeds on good and bad ground)

Thomas 9; Mark 4:3–8; Matthew 13:3–8; Luke 8:5–8; 1 Clement 24:5

17. Kingdom is like a mustard seed

Thomas 20; Mark 4:30–32; Q (Luke 13:18–19; Matthew 13:31–33)

18. Lamp and basket

(don't hide your inner light)

Thomas 33; Mark 4:21; Q (Luke 8:16, 11:33; Matthew 5:15)

19. Serpents and doves

(be clever and gentle)

Thomas 39; P. Oxyrhynchus 655; Matthew 10; Gospel of the Nazarenes 7; Ignatius letter to Polycarp

20. Who have receive, those without deprived

(the rich get richer)

Thomas 41; Mk 4:25; Q (Luke 19:26; Matthew 25:29)

21. Blessed are the poor

(fortunate, close to the kingdom)

Thomas 54; Q (Luke 6:20; Matthew 5:3); James 2:5; Polycarp letter

HIGHEST RANKED SAYINGS FROM THE JESUS SEMINAR

(21 sayings that likely came from Jesus)

The Jesus Seminar scholars analyze each saying attributed to Jesus and vote on authenticity. The 21 sayings below received a ranking of 70% or higher as likely Jesus sayings. For a complete listing and explanation see *The Five Gospels*, by Robert W. Funk and Roy W. Hoover (Scribner, 1993).

1. Turn the other cheek
Q (Luke 6:29; Matthew 5:39)
2. If someone asks for your coat, give your shirt also
Q (Luke 6:29; Matthew 5:40)
3. Blessed are the poor
Thomas 54; Q (Matthew 5:3; Luke 6:20)
4. Go the second mile
Q (Matthew 5:41)
5. Love your enemies
Q (Luke 6:27-35; Matthew 5:44)
6. The kingdom is like leaven
(common saying outside the Jesus tradition)
Thomas 96; Q (Luke 13:20–21, Matthew 13:33)
7. Coin, Caesar, and God
(give to God what belongs to God)
Thomas 100; Mark 12:17; Luke 20:25; Matthew 22:21; Egerton Gospel 3:1–6
8. Give to one who begs from you
Thomas 95; Q (Luke 6:30; Matthew 5:42); Didache 1:5
9. Good Samaritan
Luke 10:30–35
10. Blessed are the hungry
Thomas 69; Q (Luke 6:21, Matthew 5:6)
11. Blessed those who weep
Q (Luke 6:21; Matthew 5:4); Dialogue of the Saviour 13; John 16:20–22

12. The shrewd manager (settling his master's debts)

Luke 16:1–8

13. Vineyard labourers (the first will be last)

Matthew 20:1–15

14. Abba, Father (prayer)

Q (Matthew 6; Luke 11)

15. The kingdom is like a mustard seed

Thomas 20; Mark 4:30–32; Q (Luke 13; Matthew 13)

16. Don't worry

(trust in God, look at the birds and lilies)

Thomas 36; Q (Luke 12; Matthew 6)

17. Lost coin

(woman will search for her lost coin): Luke 15:8–9

18. Foxes have dens

(a son of Adam has nowhere to rest his head) This saying is similar to both Buddhist and Taoist sayings.

Thomas 86; Q (Luke 9:58; Matthew 8:20)

19. A prophet gets no respect at home

The one saying that the John gospel shares with Thomas, Luke, Matthew, and Mark.

Thomas 31; Luke 4:24; Matthew 13:57; Mark 6:4; John 4:44

20. A friend visits at midnight

(parable to illustrate "seek and you'll receive")

Luke 11:5–8

21. You cannot serve two masters

(money and God)

Thomas 47; Q (Luke 16:13; Matthew 6:24)

2.
MISCONCEPTIONS: SAYINGS AND IDEAS THAT JESUS DID NOT ORIGINATE OR SAY

Three categories describe sayings erroneously attributed to Jesus:
1. common wisdom and lore that Jesus or gospel authors borrowed
2. ancient cosmologies, theologies, and philosophies adopted by Judaism and Christianity, and
3. later doctrines formulated by Greek and Latin Christians and attributed to Jesus.

COMMON SAYINGS AND LORE THAT JESUS LIKELY BORROWED

Jesus probably repeated these ideas gleaned from his cultural environment.

■ The Golden Rule, a common ancient aphorism, is mentioned by Confucius in *The Analects*, by Herodotus in *The Histories*, in the Hindu *Mahabharata*, and in the Zoroastrian *Dadistan-I-Dinik*. Jesus likely heard the Jewish Hillel version: "What is hateful to you, do not unto your neighbour." Jesus makes it positive, as recorded by Matthew in the Sermon on the Mount: "Treat people the way you want them to treat you."

■ "Love your enemy" is a universal concept, recorded in Akkadian, Buddhist, and pagan traditions. The Taoist version states simply, "Return love for hatred."

- "Know yourself" was inscribed over the entrance to the Apollo temple at Delphi. The aphorism is attributed to Socrates, Thales, Pythagoras, and others. Buddha said, "Know your own mind."
- "Don't judge others" belongs to common wisdom. Hillel says (*Avot* 2, 4) "Judge not your neighbour until you are in his place."
- "A good tree is known by its fruits" reflects common proverbial wisdom.
- "Healthy people don't need a doctor, the sick do," originates with the Cynic sages.

ANCIENT CONCEPTS ADOPTED BY JUDAISM OR CHRISTIANITY

Writers often attributed theological and cosmological concepts from Egypt, Babylon, and Persia to Jesus. The following doctrines entered Judaism from Egyptian or Zoroastrian tradition after Persian King Cyrus began to influence Jewish scriptures. Jesus did not originate these ideas:

- angels
- a trinity of deities
- the end of the world
- resurrection of the dead
- Judgment Day
- eternal life
- paradise in heaven
- a fiery hell, devils, and demons
- ritual requirements through priests to attain heaven

- purification by water, baptism
- redemption of sins only through priests and sacrifice
- a transcendent messianic saviour
- son of God, human children of the deities: Osiris, Horus, Mithras, Hercules, Bacchus, Pythagoras, Attis, Tammuz, Thor (Baltic), Beddru (Japan), and others
- virgin mother: Horus, Attis, Mithras, Adonis, Dionysus, Krishna, and others
- divine birth on the solstice, or three days after (December 25)
- A single, male deity: This concept comes from Egypt and Persia, associated with single, male, all-powerful kings. The Old Testament mentions several Hebrew deities: El, Elohim, El Elyon (the Most High), Aveer, Shaddai, and the god of Moses, YHVH. Jesus mentions El, Elohim, Abba, and the Most High. El is a Canaanite god associated with a council of deities, including his consort Asherah, Queen of Heaven. Peasant Jews in northern Israel were not necessarily monotheistic, and Jesus never mentions YHVH or declares that there is only one deity.
- Eucharist meal, wine and bread as the blood and body of a saviour: Jesus does not proclaim this idea. Gospel writers borrowed the Last Supper story directly from Persian Mithraism. Jesus' ritual meal honoured communal sharing not the consumption of an embodied deity.
- Many Bible stories – the Last Supper, raising of Lazarus, twelve disciples – are borrowed from Egyptian and Persian sources. For more details about ancient mythology in the Old and New Testament, see *The Pagan Christ*, Tom

Harpur (Thomas Allen, 2004); and *Ancient Christian Gospels: Their History and Development*, Helmut Koester (Trinity Press, 1990).

LATER CHRISTIAN DOCTRINES

- Jesus as a messiah ("Christos"): Jesus does not make this claim. Paul introduces the idea.
- Blood atonement: Jesus dying for sins is a later Roman idea. Jesus associated forgiveness with forgiving others. Original sin: Jewish theology does not include this doctrine, and Jesus never mentions it. The idea originated in the fourth century with Augustine.
- To gain heaven, believe in Jesus as messiah: Jesus does not say this. The concept begins with Paul, and was later developed by Roman and Protestant churches.
- Male disciples and priests: Later Greek and Latin Christian writers adopted this patriarchal idea, expunged goddesses and priestesses, denounced women in churches, and slandered Mary Magdalene. Jesus included Mary and other women among his closest disciples.
- Greek idioms: Evidence shows that Roman gospel authors searched Jewish scriptures to make the new Roman religion appear foretold, but they relied on Greek translations. They expose their deception by putting Greek idioms on the lips of Jesus, including the un-Jewish "I am" statements *(ego eimi)* in the John gospel. Jesus spoke Aramaic and taught by his own authority and knowledge, not by appealing to scriptures, especially in Greek translation.

■ For a survey of gospel sources, later editing, and doubtful attributions to Jesus, see *Misquoting Jesus*, Bart D. Ehrman (Harper, 2005); *The Canon of the New Testament: Its Origin, Development and Significance*, Bruce M. Metzger (Clarendon Press, 1987); and *The Five Gospels*, Robert W. Funk and Roy W. Hoover (Scribner, 1993).

3.
SOURCES

THE COMPLETE GOSPELS

We possess no Aramaic, Hebrew, or first-century New Testament manuscripts. The earliest Greek manuscripts employ different words, verses, and chapters. English editions of the Bible suffer from erroneous sources, later redaction, and poor translation. Beyond the popular gospels, some 200 sources – gospels, sayings collections, dialogues, commentaries, and other accounts – contribute to an understanding of what Jesus (the historical Yeshua) might have said. The following sources were used for this book.

Karen L. King, *The Gospel of Mary of Magdala*, (Polebridge, 2003): The Mary gospel merits particular focus due to the purging of the feminine voice in the historical record.

Peter Kirby, comp., *Early Christian Writings* at www.earlychristianwritings.com: Alternative translations and commentary for each of 155 significant texts from the first three centuries after the life of Jesus.

Marvin Meyer, *The Gospel Thomas* (Harper, 1992): The Thomas gospel stands as the earliest known collection of sayings from Jesus, Yeshua, the beginning of the historical record.

R. J. Miller, ed., *The Complete Gospels* (Polebridge, 1992): Includes the New Testament and 17 additional gospels and fragments, including Thomas, Mary, Ebionites,

Nazoreans, Hebrews, Dialogue of the Saviour, the Gospel of Peter, and others.

Bruce M. Metzger and Roland E. Murphy, eds., *The New Oxford Annotated Bible New Revised Standard Version* (Oxford University, 1973, 1994): A reliable modern translation with notes explaining the problems, uncertainties, and history of revisions. A panel of 34 historians and text analysts worked with Metzger and Murphy.

James M. Robinson, ed., *The Nag Hammadi Library* (Harper & Row, 1988): The complete contents of the 13 books found near Nag Hammadi, Egypt, in 1945, plus four manuscripts from Oxyrhynchus, Egypt. The 47 texts include the gospels of Thomas, Mary, Philip, Egyptians, Pistis Sophia, "The Thunder: Perfect Mind," and others.

James Strong, *The New Strong's Exhaustive Concordance of the Bible* (Thomas Nelson, 1991): The source for definitions of Hebrew and Greek words used in the Bible, available online at www.htmlbible.com.

A JEWISH JESUS

Géza Vermes, *Jesus the Jew* (Fortress Press, 1981), and *Jesus in His Jewish Context* (Fortress Press, 2003).

E. P. Sanders, *Jesus and Judaism* (Fortress Press, 1987).

THE HISTORICAL JESUS

John Dominic Crossan, *The Historical Jesus* (Harper Collins, 1992); *Jesus: A Revolutionary Biography* (Harper Collins, 1994); and *Excavating Jesus*, with Jonathan L. Reed (HarperCollins, 2001).

Burton Mack, *Christian Myth* (Continuum, 2001); and *Who Wrote the New Testament?* (Harper, 1996).
Norman Perrin, *Rediscovering the Teaching of Jesus* (HarperCollins, 1976).
E. P. Sanders, *The Historical Figure of Jesus* (Penguin, 1996).
David F. Strauss, *The Life of Jesus Critically Examined* (1835).
Albert Schweitzer, *The Quest of the Historical Jesus* (1909).
Gerd Theissen, *The Historical Jesus: A Comprehensive Guide* (Fortress Press, 1998).

WRITERS RECONCILING CHRISTIAN FAITH WITH A HISTORICAL JESUS

Marcus J. Borg, *Jesus: The Life, Teaching, and Relevance of a Religious Revolutionary* (HarperCollins, 2006).
N. T. Wright, *The Original Jesus: The Life and Vision of a Revolutionary* (Eerdmans, 1997).

TRANSLATIONS

All quotations attributed to Jesus, including the earliest Greek versions, reflect reconstructed, paraphrased renderings. Unless otherwise mentioned, quotations from the Old and New Testament rely on the *Oxford Annotated Bible: New Revised Standard Version* and "Scholars Version" translations. The renderings in this book sometimes merge sources based on a review of the earliest known Hebrew or Greek originals.

ABOUT THE AUTHOR

Rex Weyler is the critically acclaimed author of *Blood of the Land*, which was nominated for a Pulitzer Prize, and *Greenpeace: The Inside Story*, which was a finalist for the Shaughnessy Cohen Award for Political Non-Fiction, the Hubert Evans Award for Non-Fiction, and was named one of the best books of 2004 by the *Ottawa Citizen*, Halifax Public Libraries, *Publisher's Weekly*, and the *Seattle Post-Intelligencer*. He co-authored the self-discovery classic *Chop Wood, Carry Water: A Guide to Finding Spiritual Fulfillment in Everyday Life*. He is also the author of the brilliant synthesis of the work of international Bible scholars, *The Jesus Sayings: The Quest for His Authentic Message*, from which the present work is drawn. His photography and essays have appeared in such publications as the *New York Times*, *Smithsonian*, *Rolling Stone*, *New Age Journal*, and *National Geographic*. He lives on Cortes Island in British Columbia, Canada.

Other Books in the **Manifest** series

Thomas Lombardo
THE PURSUIT OF VIRTUE
The Path to
a Good Future

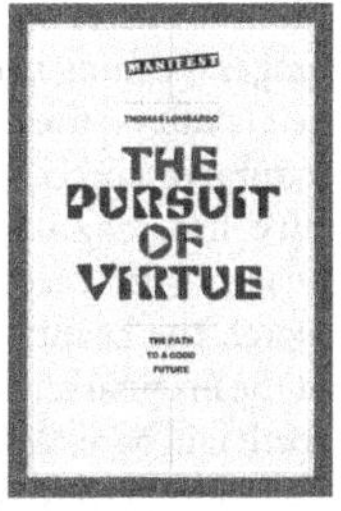

The world is too much with us. It was 1802 when English Romantic poet William Wordsworth remarked that humanity was wasting its energy on the quest for material acquisition.

Centuries later, we are arguably worse off – with growing numbers suffering from maladies ranging from affluenza to social media addiction, narcissism, and worse. As respected futurist Thomas Lombardo puts it, "We are becoming lost and forlorn, drowning in an overpowering present."

In this short insightful book he calls us to instead create new forms of inspiration that will guide us to wisdom.

"Building on knowledge of the past and the possibilities of the future, it is important to develop an informed and inspiring grand narrative of the intersection of human life, nature, and the cosmos."

ISBN 978-1-77343-152-9
4.25" x 6.25" | 128 pages | Paperback | $12.95

Other Books in the **Manifest** series

Warren Johnson

FOR EVERYTHING A SEASON

The Wisdom of Traditional Values
in Turbulent Times

The pursuit of wealth and power no longer sustains us. Our economy has been built on the heavy-handed use of natural resources, and even though nature has magnificent recuperative powers, the recovery is unlikely to match the beauty and the wholeness of the original environment. With this truth laid bare, Warren Johnson offers up a new path to deep inner prosperity based on one of the oldest and most successful concepts the world over – The Golden Rule.

"Right to the land was secured through good husbandry. It was assumed that concern for one's children and their children was the strongest basis for preserving the land's productivity. How different such a society would be compared to the one we live in. True, it would not be as productive in the short term, but we have already seen that our current pattern of maximizing profits and feeding short-term self-interests has only sowed seeds of dissent. Instead, the biblical way would be a better one. It would not only be sustainable, but the thrust of each day would shift from wealth creation to healthy, happy interpersonal relationships."

ISBN 978-1-77343-166-6

4.25" x 6.25" | 96 pages | Paperback | $12.95

Other Books in the **Manifest** series

Walter G. Moss

IN THE FACE OF FEAR

On Laughing All the Way
to Wisdom

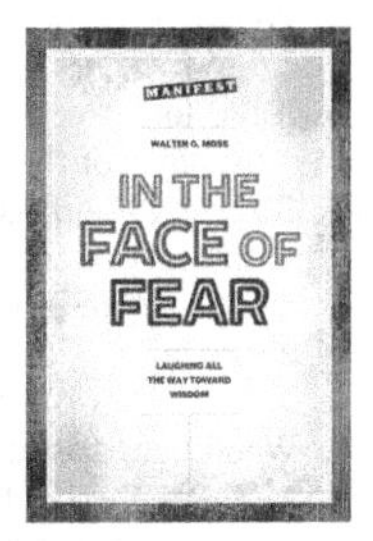

In today's click-happy world, humour all too often strikes at the heart of the other. It's about laughing at another's expense, guffawing in superiority, and generally casting our eye on other people's failings.

Walter G. Moss reminds us that this social habit is a long way from what humour once was – a method to maintain perspective, and to look at the world in such a way that we can overcome whatever hits us.

Life can be funny – not just other people's lives, but our own lives. Walter says this very ability is a sign of both maturity and of wisdom. When we laugh at ourselves, all the world can laugh with us.

ISBN 978-1-77343-160-4
4.25" x 6.25" | 96 pages | Paperback | $12.95

WOOD LAKE

Imagining, living, and telling the faith story.

WOOD LAKE IS THE FAITH STORY COMPANY.

It has told

- the story of the seasons of the earth, the people of God, and the place and purpose of faith in the world;
- the story of the faith journey, from birth to death;
- the story of Jesus and the churches that carry his message.

Wood Lake has been telling stories for more than 35 years. During that time, it has given form and substance to the words, songs, pictures, and ideas of hundreds of storytellers.

Those stories have taken a multitude of forms – parables, poems, drawings, prayers, epiphanies, songs, books, paintings, hymns, curricula – all driven by a common mission of serving those on the faith journey.